Cracked Pots

Shunned, Shattered
and
Saved by Grace

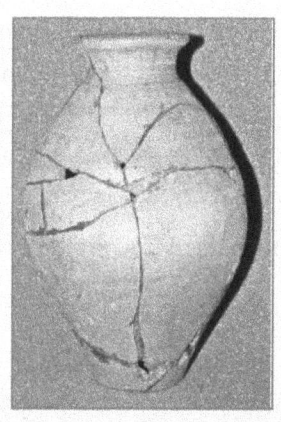

*A Memoir
Based on the Transformed Life of
Elder Mae Fogle*

Unless otherwise indicated, all Scripture is taken from the Life Application Study Bible, (New Living Translation, Second Edition by Tyndale House Publishing).

§

All rights reserved. No part of this publication may be reproduced, stored in a retrieval system, or transmitted in any form, for example: electronic, photocopy or in recording devices without the prior written permission of the author. The only exception is brief references for educational purposes.

CRACKED POTS is dedicated to
my mother and father.
Further, it is a clarion call to families everywhere.
Please, let's begin to love, nurture
and encourage our babies.

The Spirit of the Lord is upon me, because he hath anointed me to preach the gospel to the poor; he hath sent me to heal the brokenhearted, to preach deliverance to the captives, and recovering of sight to the blind, to set at liberty them that are bruised,

Luke 4:18

"I didn't know when.
I didn't even know how.
But, I knew
the tears I shed would heal my wounds
so that I might make
someone smile one day.
I knew deep in my soul
that I would live
to give someone hope.
The Elders told me so
long ago."

~ by Elder Mae Fogle

ACKNOWLEDGMENTS

First and foremost, I thank God for impressing upon my heart to share my story through poetry and prose. By the Holy Spirit's guidance, I pray that just as I was delivered out of a life of chaos and self-destruction, others will likewise understand they can also find deliverance through forgiveness and a genuine trust in God.

I would also like to express heartfelt thanks to the many wonderful individuals who gave unselfishly of your time, encouraged, nurtured, prayed, and typed drafts to help with this project. Your names are too numerous to mention but you know that I thank all of you from the depth and breadth of my heart. Your valuable advice and knowledge was priceless. For every second, minute or hour you took out of your busy schedules to read and re-read drafts, I thank you. Had it not been for your incredible support and input, none of what I have desired to do for so long would have happened. In truth, my writings would still be gathering dust upon the shelves.

My appreciation is deeper than mere words can ever express. My prayers, however, are heartfelt that God richly blesses each one of you in very special ways. You have definitely been a blessing to me!

Foreword

CRACKED POTS has always been a lifelong dream until I finally decided to write out my dream in order to purge body, spirit and soul of a history of bad memories. I began to give serious attention to it over seven years ago. It is a type of detoxification that chronicles a life of dysfunction, near death and the miraculous transformation of a little girl lost-me. Once the scales were lifted from my eyes, I thought it was my reasonable service to share my story with the world. I felt a duty to testify to as many as will hear that everything is possible if one only believes. It wasn't an easy process to get to this point but it became possible once I finally put all my trust in Almighty God.

All of what I have shared is true and based on oral history and personal reflections of my youth. I have also included a few of the poems I composed, some of which can be put to song. They evolved from the many different and trying stages of my life.

Long before I put pen to paper to begin *CRACKED POTS*, I shared my life trials with so many people who often told me that I needed to write a book. For a long time, I dismissed that idea. Why? Well, I didn't believe anyone would be interested. I wasn't a star. In fact, I wasn't a prominent figure by any measure. Who would care about the devastating life experiences of an unknown little girl named Mae Fogle

Those who understand know that this is how the enemy keeps us from achieving our divine purpose in life. Clearly, I was a victim to Satan's distractions for a long time. In fact, the whispers became a nagging voice in my head suggesting things like: Do you really want to be that transparent? Do you really want people to know the real deal about your life? Foolishly, I was shackled to these demeaning thoughts for many years. Meantime, my notes for *CRACKED POTS* gathered more and more dust.

Many years passed and a dear friend of mine said, "Mae", I heard about your story. You need to tell it." I remained doubtful. A short while later, another affirmation came to me by way of a televangelist who said, "You need to tell your story." I continued to drag my feet.

Finally, a resounding message came to me in black and white via my daily devotional. What I read that day seemed to shout, "TELL YOUR STORY, WOMAN!" I figured this was God's way of telling me to get to work and write. I did. Thus, began the journey of gathering my notes out of the dust pile and organizing them to tell my story.

Thanks to that still, small voice that leads us all into the glorious light. All Glory to God for putting the right people and situations in my path to bring this to fruition.

Table of Contents

In the Beginning 11

Momma: A Cracked Pot Too! 18

Daddy Unveiled: A Great Provider and A Cracked Pot, Too! 24

Looking for Love In All the Wrong Places 28

If Not One Thing, It Was Another: Secrets, Secrets and More Secrets 41

Another Blow To the Little Cracked Pot "Second Crack" 47

Help! 65

The Gang's All Here! 68

Homelessness 70

Daddy's Gone. Momma, Too! 75

Church: Will The Real Christians please Stand Up! 81

If I can't find help in the Church Then Where? 86

My Earth Angel: Momma Davis 97

You Were There All the Time 121

Epilogue 133

IN THE BEGINNING

Can a person walk forward while looking backwards at the same time? Yes, if looking back means finding answers to questions that have haunted an individual for a lifetime. By looking back, a key detail became crystal clear to me. I was trained to fight, literally and figuratively, for my life every since the day I was born.

At birth, I was given the name Mae. I entered this world prematurely in Freeman Hospital (originally, Freedmen's Hospital that was established by Howard University for Black Civil War Veterans in the 1800s). My mother's pregnancy with me lasted seven short months. I was told she was confined to bed rest during the entire time. No one ever told me why and, once I was old enough, I don't recall ever asking.

What I do remember is daddy telling me that I was a tiny baby. He said I was so small that I could fit just as easily inside a coffee pot as into the palm of his hands. Maybe it could have been explained better but daddy did the best he could with a limited vocabulary. Because I was premature, he said the veins in my brain were visible and bulged at the top of my head. Again, based on his graphic description, I must have been a frightening specimen to cast your eyes upon.

Anyway, I eventually began to develop after months of being incubated. My frail body fought to stay alive even then. At some point, I was finally healthy enough to be released to go home with my parents. I was told my mother really didn't know how to care for me when I came home. My dad took care of everything. In fact, one day when he went to work, my mother called him in a panic. *"Please hurry home," she said. "The child done stopped breathing and turned another color."* I was a very fair-skinned child, which would become a thorn later in life.

Now, I don't exactly know why or how this next thing happened on the day my daddy rushed home, but I was told as soon as his feet crossed the threshold and he picked me up, both my complexion and breathing returned to normal. More amazing, his show of affection would eventually cause my mother to loathe me.

Another time, there was a problem with the development of my feet. Daddy was the one who took me to the doctor. I wasn't walking yet but the bones in my feet were clearly showing signs of some type of deformity. The doctor prescribed corrective shoes to address the problem. I must have resembled a baby *Forest Gump* in those special shoes. But that didn't matter. Daddy was taking care of me.

In fact, when I was old enough, he told me that he took those preventative steps when he did so that whenever I did begin to walk, I wouldn't have any problems. As far as I was concerned, I thought he was the smartest man on earth. And, yes, I thought I was 'daddy's little girl'. That was the first and perhaps the last time in my youth that I can remember ever feeling so happy.

When I look back, especially at my odd childhood and upbringing, and my mother's strained pregnancy with me, I often wonder if those conditions affected my mental stability. I say this because around four years old, I remember a strange shift in my thoughts and personality. One day, while playing with my doll baby, I decided to snap her head off. I don't know why. I just did. What's more surprising, I buried the head in the backyard. Some years later, around nine or ten years old, I had these flower seeds. Rather than plant them in the backyard (like my doll baby's head), I threw the seeds randomly over the ground. To my surprise they grew into such beautiful flowers—yellow, blue, green, purple and orange. They were lovely! I couldn't believe it. Why would I plant the seeds and bury my doll's head? I started to wonder if something was wrong with me.

Even though I was a young girl, I thought those acts were weird. In truth, I thought I was crazy. After all, that's what people around me were saying all the time. *"Something's wrong with that girl,"* they'd say. *"She's a bad seed."* Clearly, something was broken inside of me. Something was missing from my life. All the signs were there but no one bothered to address them in a constructive way. No one showed any real concern. At this stage in my life, I didn't know that I was already showing the first signs of a cracked pot.

As shared earlier, I was a very fair-skinned child with long, sandy hair and was blessed with greyish blue eyes. As a young, African-American girl back in the day, this made me a target of ridicule.

Often, the kids would shout, "What color are you? Are you Black or white?" They would make fun and laugh at me. Of course, in my mind the only option I thought I had was to retaliate. So I fought them—all the time, every day. If they harassed me about anything, I would fight. Sadly, no one had ever instilled the fact that I was wonderful in my own skin. I didn't have anyone to tell me to walk away from name-calling or any such nonsense. Neither did I have anyone to praise my uniqueness or educate me on self-confidence. I did, however, receive an education in the culture of combat and that's what I did. In fact, fighting became a lifetime occupation. As I grew older, that's all I continued to do. Without fear or hesitation, I would fight men. I got in tussles with women. I didn't understand that this was learned behavior until I'd spent two-thirds of my life in unnecessary turmoil.

After years of childhood disappointments and dysfunction, I grew numb. I felt as though I would never amount to anything. I felt dumb (or so I thought). My life seemed so sad and bleak at points that I seriously considered taking my own life. It was just that bad.

No child should ever consider this as an option. Sadly, I did because in many ways I was lost and misguided by a number of cracked pots that, quite honestly, didn't know any better themselves.

Some of it began when I was in elementary school. I was labeled a slow learner. Because of this, I always found it more comfortable to sit in the back of the classroom. Mind you, I wasn't dumb. I just didn't have anyone to encourage my brilliance. When I was a little older, I remember applying for a job but didn't get it. To a large degree, that hurt. On another level, not getting that job only served to crush by self-esteem and confirm what I had always thought—I really wasn't smart enough. I became depressed which led to other frightening thoughts. I felt lost and alone. Topping that, I felt unwanted by my family.

Long before I was influenced by the world, my mother and I were not getting along at all. I don't think I was quite ten years old but I sensed that she was distancing herself from me. A child can feel detachment. In truth, the word that actually came to mind was resentment. It seemed as though she didn't like the relationship I had with my dad. Because he showered me with love throughout my early years, I honestly believe my mom felt as though I was robbing her of his love and devotion. I was *their* child. My dad was just being a father. All I wanted from my mother was the same kind of love. But I didn't get it. Much later, it became clear that she was basically transferring hurt from her past on to me. There we were—one cracked pot caring and co-existing with another cracked pot. Following is a perfect example.

Once, when I was alone with my mother, she called me over to comb my hair. Daddy had gone to work. As I mentioned earlier, I had very long, curly hair. My mom would comb my hair as hard and rough as she could. When I would squirm or try to pull away, she would whack me in the head with the brush, comb or her heavy hand. WHAP! Naturally, I would cry out and say that I was going to tell my father. *"He's what's wrong with you now," said my mother.* She thought my dad had spoiled me rotten. In his own way, I can say that he did spoil me. But that's what parents do. In my mother's case, she resented every bit of it and whenever we were alone, she would seize every opportunity to make me pay for his open affection. Sadly, I paid deeply for being *daddy's little girl*.

MOMMA: A CRACKED POT TOO!

To understand my mother and our relationship, I must first share some underlying personal issues she possessed of her own. In other words, it is important that I expose her *death pain,* so to speak. She didn't have an easy young life. Her adult life was turbulent, too. In fact, for most of her life she held a one-way bus ticket to hell until finally boarding the hallelujah train. Everything changed from that point.

Once I was old enough to understand, I learned that when my mother was a young girl, my grandmother whose name was Lottie B handed her off to others. Why? Well, my mother was pregnant. During this era, it was thought that a young girl wasn't supposed to have children until she was married. For all intents and purposes, it was considered taboo in cultures of old if not a total disgrace to the girl's family if she did find herself in a motherly way.

Anyway, Grandma Lottie found out that my mom was pregnant; she gave my mom child away—just like that. No questions. No consoling. No offers of help. I never knew who impregnated my mom or under what circumstances she became pregnant. I was told that she was simply passed from one person to another for a good portion of her young life. I would imagine she felt abandoned, too. I guess this also contributed to her hard-hearted attitude about a lot of things.

I never knew the economic status of my mother's family but based on the few crumbs of information shared, I believe they were a struggling southern family. Once, my mom told me she had to wear sackcloth and hand-me-downs as a child. Once she was old enough, I understand she fled the south, migrating to Washington, D.C. This is where she and my dad met. They didn't marry right away but I didn't know about that until I was much older. Eventually, they married but there were so many secrets between them. Nevertheless, daddy stuck by my mom's side. I never understood why. I guess he must have really loved her.

I'm not certain how far she went in school but according to oral history, she did receive some education. She also proved to be a very hard worker. Dad had a very good job and was an engineer by trade. I understand he told her once that she didn't have to work because he could and would provide for his family. Unfortunately, as a stay-at-home mom, my mom was left to indulge in some very bad vices that would prove detrimental to her, and me, for a good portion of our lives.

To state it another way, my mother was a hell raiser, heavy drinker and a combative woman who would argue and fight at the drop of a dime. Her family had been the same way. I was told she tried to smoke cigarettes, too, but that vice didn't agree with her. That was the one thing that never developed into a habit for her. Good thing. There were so many other things I often wished hadn't agreed with her.

It never took much to get mom riled up. She was a hefty woman who weighed close to three hundred pounds and once that one nerve was struck, she was a mighty force. As the story goes, it took about a dozen policemen to restrain her one time. Another time, when I was a little girl, I caught a glimpse of my dad's arms. There were deep, ugly cuts all over them like they'd been pressed through a meat grinder.

I remember asking daddy why his arms looked like that but he never said a thing. I knew he hadn't cut himself.

On another occasion, my mom told me about a co-worker, a man named Fess. He flirted with her constantly. I understand she asked Fess to stop but he wouldn't. She told him she was married. Fess wouldn't stop. I don't know what my mom said and she never told me why but Fess slapped her another time. That wasn't a smart thing to do to my mom "good hair Mack" Somehow, she got her hands on a pot of boiling water, doused the man then palmed a butcher knife. In the end, Fess suffered cuts over 98% of his body! He survived but from that day forward, I was told he never approached her again.

MOMMA, WHY DO YOU HATE ME SO?

"I should have killed you while you were in my womb!" Those were words shouted from my mother's very own mouth one day. I remember being about eight or nine years old at the time. It was a short statement that consisted of only eleven words but they poisoned my soul. They struck my heart at the speed of a wrecking ball moving at 100 miles per hour. I was crushed. Why would a mother say such an ugly thing?

When I think about what she said on that day, I still cringe. Momma didn't have to wish I hadn't been born. In fact, before I had turned thirteen years of age, I was already wishing I were dead. I'd seen and experienced more than any normal child should ever have to endure over such a short life span.

From the moment she shouted those ugly words, life suddenly no longer mattered to me. I began to do everything within my powers to prove how little I regarded my life or anyone's life for that matter.

It was a sad and ugly run. And, it was dangerous. I placed myself in situations that had every potential to rob me of my life. To put it bluntly, it took years of drinking, drugs, sex, gangs, theft, prostitution, and ultimately incarceration before the scales were finally lifted from my eyes.

Even as I tried to do better, I failed over and over again until the convicting, all-powerful, third person of the Trinity, the Holy Spirit, ordered my steps.

"For he [God] did not kill me in the womb,
With my mother as my grave; but, her womb
enlarged forever."
~ Jeremiah 20:17 (NIV)

DADDY UNVEILED: A GREAT PROVIDER AND A CRACKED POT, TOO!

One day out of the blue, one of my cousins shared a shocking secret about my dad. *"Your dad's a rolling stone,"* Art said. At first, I didn't understand. Then, Art began to rattle off details about my dad's infidelity. No way, I thought. My dad loved my mom. He would never be unfaithful. I had never given any thought to my dad having other women in his life. There were never any signs. He had shown complete respect for my mom and his household. As time passed, I did learn that he was indeed sowing his oats elsewhere. In fact, I was told there were many women from all walks of life who loved on my dad.

My dad was tall, lean and a sharp dresser. He was a special handsome with fine features and the finest grade of hair I had ever seen on a man. Add charming to these, and I could understand how women might get all *bug-eyed* over him. It was no secret that my mom could be a tyrant. Although he never confessed it, I knew my mom had left her marks of vengeance on his arms. Maybe this was why my dad

cheated. I don't know and I'm not trying to justify it. Perhaps he did it to maintain his sanity. Living with my mom was no picnic but deep down I still sensed he loved her.

Dad tolerated a lot from my mom but he was not the type of man who would ever raise his hands to her. That just wasn't his style. Neither did he ever say a negative word about my mother. I couldn't understand that at all.

I remember asking my dad on several occasions, *"Why won't you leave her?"* I remember my dad saying, *"No, Mae, your mother has problems."* I guess by staying with her, even with his secrets, he thought he could love her problems (or better, death pain) away. I'm beginning to think my father's a cracked pot, too.

My dad didn't receive a lot of formal education. As a matter of fact, he was mostly self-educated. Still, he was gifted with his hands and smart. I mean super smart. He was especially sharp when it came to money matters.

As shared before, he was an engineer by trade. Because of his skill set, my dad once taught at an engineering trade center to help immigrant workers learn a vocation. He helped so many people and enjoyed doing so. He had an engaging personality and was loved and highly regarded for the excellent work he did at the center. Over the course of his career, he was also privileged to be exposed to some very important people in his field.

Another time, my dad told me about a job interview where he did something very unique. It was unthought-of during his era and especially for a Black man. For a job interview, he built a model boiler room out of Popsicle sticks. Go figure. He got the job! I told you, my dad was a very smart man. He loved his family and took very good care of us. He made it possible for us to live in nice homes in upper-middle class neighborhoods, some of them near the Georgetown area in Washington, D.C. We always had food on the table, nice clothes and shoes to wear. My dad also provided mom with the best of everything.

One time when my mother was having trouble with her teeth, dad paid $1,000.00 for dentures. He even went so far as to have gold fillings put in them. Of course, now I know that the extra money came from one of the two settlements, both of which came about after two, near-death situations for me. More on that a little later, however.

Misfortune came to my dad one day in the boiler room of our house. One of his fingers was accidentally severed from his hand. After this, he found it difficult to continue in his trade. As time passed, his overall health also began to worsen. Soon, he'd have to spend his last days in his hometown of Dallas, Texas. In the meantime. . .

LOOKING FOR LOVE IN ALL THE WRONG PLACES

I always felt something was missing on the inside of me. I thought that void was the love of a man. When I went searching for it (or him), what I found was more of what I already felt--emptiness. There were a few men who were genuinely interested in me. Some, I truly believed might have been a great mate but I didn't have enough sense or any positive examples to know the good ones from the bad ones during my lost years. There was no measuring stick to gauge character. Sound judgment was not a priority during my years in the wilderness. After being showcased on a sandbox and made to dance provocatively before old, perverted men as a child, I thought this was what big girls were supposed to do.

Before I reached my early-teens I was already a fully developed child with breasts the size of cantaloupes. By all standards, I was pretty, shapely and trained in promiscuity. I became a showpiece. "Look man, ain't she pretty?" one of them, a man named Jake, once said. Normally, all this meant was that I was going to be boxed in—Jake planned to keep me to himself. Another one, John, kept me on lockdown in a padlocked room with a bedpan to relieve myself. I became involved with yet another man who would cry after we had sexual relations. Everyone just called him Q for short. "You better not leave me," Q said one day. He'd say it again in case I hadn't heard the first time. "You better not leave me. If you do, I'll kill you." I narrowly escaped that situation.

Then, there was the sadomasochistic nut. His name was Stoney and his demeanor fit his name. I knew my life was on the line when I first entered his home; yet, I entered anyway. He was a trick. I needed money. It was a dark and scary place that smelled of death. If I hadn't thought of a quick escape, I would have been an addition to his collection of skulls and bones, snakes as well as all the other craziness I saw in his home.

This was during a dark season of my life when I worked the streets and bars to survive. Anyway, after a quick assessment of this man's insanity, a base instinct told me to run and I did. I truly believe I survived that situation by an inch of my life.

Finally, the worst of all possible encounters was

the time I was solicited by a man of the cloth. He was a Pastor. It was during the time I worked the streets. My friend and I recognized him from the neighborhood.

I don't know why I was surprised but he was about as perverted as they come. Not only did he engage in sexual relations with young girls but also he delighted in these relations during their menstrual cycles. He was also an exhibitionist. Clearly, he was a wicked man.
Even if he lied about being a pastor, he was still deranged beyond belief!

MY WILDERNESS

Growing up, I was regularly exposed to the grey, hazy fumes of smoked-filled rooms as the adults puffed their lives away. I would sneak cigarettes from the packs my daddy left laying around. By nine years of age, I had begun to smoke like everyone else. By nine and a half, I received my first taste of alcohol. In fact, my father's brother introduced me to my first experience with alcohol. I remember it like it was yesterday. It was Old Taylor mixed with water and warmed up so that it would go down easy. My uncle made it seem fun, calling it "hot toddies". So now, long before I had reached the age of ten, I had acquired the taste for alcohol and nicotine. Far worse, I witnessed my elders engaged in sexual relations. That, too, would soon become a way of life for me as well. Clearly, I was on that slippery slope of destruction.

Just as often as I witnessed their smoking, I was exposed to their excessive drinking too. My mother drank, remember. Her favorite, in fact, was Gin, no chaser. After getting her fill of liquor, she fought. Her scars became mine. Her internal pain became my personal hurt. An internal dislike of self became and outward hatred of me. Daddy's silence through it all was frustrating. I felt abandoned even from him. Sometimes, I just prayed to forget. Sometimes, I prayed for death. Anything was better than what I was experiencing as a child.

I tried to erase the ugliness from my memory but that was like putting a one-inch Band-Aid on a twelve-inch wound. In time, the ugliness seeps through and stains one's clothing and character. What's a child to do? Well, I became my environment. It wasn't so outrageous. I lived my life as I'd seen others live--on the wild side.

"I have not come to arouse and invite and call the righteous,
but the erring ones (those not free from sin) to repentance
[to change their minds for the better and heartily to amend their ways,
with abhorrence of
their past sins]."
~ Luke 5:32 (Amplified)

Free Me!
§

*I've been up
I've been down.
An entire life
turned upside down.
Everywhere I go,
people telling me no.
Just where, I ask,
can I go?
Really, can I ever be free?
Somebody,
tell me please.
Where can I go?
from all . . . all this misery?*

LORD, HELP ME PLEASE!

My life went from cracked to fractured to a million shattered pieces. The nightmare seemed as though it would never end. I was at odds with my mother. Other family members found it easier to shun me rather than help shape me into a normal child. I'd dropped out of junior high school. I was hooked on drugs, alcohol and so many other vices. I became the object of depraved individuals whose pleasures were to make a profit off of my body, a body that had developed far quicker than my mental state. I was drawn into prostitution by a married couple. Before I had reached the age of fifteen, I knew how to work the bars and streets better than a seasoned hustler.

Salt was added to my deepening wounds when I was raped, then became pregnant. Although the pregnancy resulted in a miscarriage, the scars of that experience never healed. The battle wounds of being shot at and stabbed served to harden me further. After this, there were the gangs. When that grew stale, theft provided the sick thrill I thought I needed. I was a certified cracked pot.

I tried to clean up my act. I sought the help of one of my siblings only to have the street call me back into its deadly web. I sought employment and found work only to be discharged because of my drinking. Finally, I sought the one place where I thought I'd find solace. I found a church family. Big mistake! There was betrayal there too. After sharing my story with so-called Christians, they began to gossip about me. Some distanced themselves from me, thinking I was some sort of disease because of the turbulent life I had lived.

Where could I go and not feel shunned, shattered and abused? The streets had betrayed me. Gang affiliation had cost me my freedom. Family had abandoned me. At a point, I was homeless and living in a women's shelter. Even that was a battlefield.

Most disturbing was how members of the church had turned their backs on me when I needed understanding and direction. *Lord, help me, please!*

So Lost
§

*Woman child
running wild
filled out in places
perverse men and
women, too.
thrown out of my home,
with no family to call
my own,
needing to earn
my keep,
I sought the streets.
Mean streets
Greedy streets
killing me softly streets.
What is a child to do?
when she's not wanted.
Where else can she go?
when there's no money?*

CALL OF THE WILD

It happened on one of those nights when a personal urge to roam the streets ruled my entire being. Against my better judgment, I told my mom that I was going out. She said, *"No you are not. You ain't going nowhere!"*

In hindsight, my first mistake was telling my mother what I was going to do. A rule of thumb is to ask, not tell. Looking back, I'm certain that my very poor choice of words contributed to our worst fight ever. But what did she expect? While she'd been doing her thing, I'd also been doing what I wanted to do for a very long time and I wasn't even legal tender.

I couldn't understand why she wanted to police me now. Put another way, she was years too late and many dollars short. Anyway, a full-blown verbal fight erupted and after that, two things happened. One sent me into a mindless rage. The other filled me with a guilt I internalized for years. It weighed heavily on my conscious.

More to the point, this particular situation erupted during one of the times I had returned home. It was after being pimped out by a man and his wife. I was young, not even thirteen years of age. I'd been in the streets, suffered a rape, miscarriage and beaten within an inch of my life. I'd been hardened.

I was determined to do my own thing. Plus, I had my own addictions by now and I needed a fix. I wasn't about to have anyone stop me, including my mother.

On the other hand, my mother had determined otherwise.

To prove her point that she ruled and her word was going to be the end all, she did what she did best. She tried to intimidate me. While I stood in total defiance, she, in the meantime, gathered up a lifetime of phlegm from deep within her body cavity. The next thing I knew, she spat directly in my face. It was a cruel act that almost cost my mother her life. I wanted to physically hurt her.

Had I followed through on that desire, it would have cost me my freedom. In truth, I wanted to kill her. To this day, I thank God for not allowing me to get my hands on a weapon.

That same night, minutes after our verbal altercation and her spitting in my face, my mother suffered a crippling stroke from which she never fully recovered. In a panic, I called my dad who rushed home from work. My mother was rushed to hospital emergency. While she survived, she became immobile from that point forward. The guilt of that nearly killed me. For years, I blamed myself for her crippling situation. What did I do to cope? I fell deeper and deeper into a troubling, dangerous lifestyle.

"There is no healing of thy bruise;
thy wound is grievous."
~ Nahum 3:19

§

"Oh, come, let us go and find them!
In the paths of death they roam;
At the close of the day, [will] be sweet to say,
'I have brought some lost one home.'"

§

Spurgeon, Charles Haddon.
Commentary on Nahum 3:4". "Spurgeon's
Verse Expositions of the Bible".
www.studylight.org/commentaries/spe/nahum-
3.html. 2011.

IF NOT ONE THING, IT WAS ANOTHER: SECRETS, SECRETS AND MORE SECRETS

There were my dad's indiscretions. My mother had some personal adventures as well. Then, there were family members who whispered about my sanity behind my back to my mother. There were so many sad, horrible and sickening things going on with my family. One of the worst and saddest times of my life occurred when my parents secretly sent my baby sister away to Texas. It was fast, quick -- no warning or discussion. That hurt me deeply. I loved my baby sister very much. In fact, I'd do anything for her, including committing murder. Yes, anyone who was a threat to her had to contend with me. For a long time, I endured the pain of her absence. I would often ask my parents why they'd sent her away. It was like talking to a brick wall. I was left to live with their sickening silence. Why had they ushered my baby sister away from the family nest?

Many years later, I learned that my baby sister, who I'll call Britany, had been sent away because a male family member had been molesting her. Of course, I wanted to know who had violated Britany. Daddy wouldn't share every detail. He was afraid that if I knew the real deal, I'd go on a manhunt for the family member who had touched my sister. Daddy was right. If I knew who had touched her inappropriately, I would have certainly ended up with blood on my hands.

As fate would have it, Britany and I were reunited some years later. It was comforting to know her life had turned out good. She had eventually gone on to graduate high school and secure a great job that allowed her to purchase her own home. *All Glory to God!* In light of the ugliness that almost wrecked her young life, I can't begin to testify of the joy I felt to learn that she had progressed so well in life. It was a long time coming but a personal joy to see that she was doing just fine!

CLEARLY, SHE'S CRAZY!

Since I had been in and out of trouble for a number of reasons for so long, my situation seemed helpless. Most times, hopeless. At some point, not only had I begun to believe the negative words I had heard spoken about me, I started to embrace and act them out in living color.

I say this because whenever my mom would take me around family members, very often I would overhear them saying awful things like: "Something is wrong with that child, Mabe." That's what family called my mother—"good-hair Mabe". Anyway, one time I heard a family member say outright, "She's a bad seed. She's crazy." When a child hears this often enough, it becomes a truth that's eventually acted out in living color.

Eventually, daddy sent me away too. I guess his thinking might have been that a move would be in my best interest. Perhaps daddy thought a different environment would help me feel better about myself. I wish that had been the solution but it wasn't. What neither he nor my mother understood was that the change had to first happen in me.

There was a great deal of truth in what other family members were saying. They just had the wrong diagnosis. It is true. I did have problems. I was an addict seasoned by the streets.

Not too long after that, I was in and out of receiving homes. From there, I was sent to a detention center in Laurel, Maryland. While in this one particular institution, I got so angry I trashed the dining room, which landed me in Washington, D.C.'s General Hospital where I was committed to the mental ward. Was I crazy? The poison that had been fed into my head and heart was finally being acted out in real life.

THE CRACKED POT IS SHATTERED
"First Crack"

We all know the saying: *When it rains, it pours.* For me, it was a non-stop hurricane. These are true accounts of two near death situations. I told you, I have been fighting for my life all my life.

We were in the area of Union Station in Washington, DC. The man who had flirted with my mom and suffered the consequences of her rage crossed our paths. They both recognized one another even years later. I remember recognizing him by his scars. I felt my mom's hand tighten around mine as he said hello. After that, he moved on down the street. I don't remember if I broke away from my mother's grasp or what but all of a sudden, I saw a taxi come careening up the street. It was moving fast. I saw it and didn't see it at the same time. I was in its path, frozen. All I remember is the silent scream in my head warning me to 'get out of the way' but my body moved in slow motion.

Before I knew it, I was flying in the air. I don't

know how high I was thrown upon impact but I was lifted completely off my feet before returning to the ground. What I do remember is that my body landed on the opposite side of the street from where my mother stood. That's as much as I have been able to recall about that ill-fated day.

When I regained consciousness, I was in Children's Hospital. I'm not certain if it had been hours or days since I'd been there but I was told that my skull had been fractured. Because of the fracture, Children's Hospital kept me under observation for a period of time.

Meanwhile, my parents received a nice monetary settlement from the accident. They never told me anything about that financial windfall until many years later.

ANOTHER BLOW TO THE LITTLE CRACKED POT *"Second Crack"*

I was beginning to think that it would be easier to just die. After all, I kept drawing near to death's door. Hardship and injury had become my best friends. In fact, they were constant companions and closer than most people have ever been.

They were there when I fell into a hole at a construction site not long after the taxicab incident.

I was almost ten years old and on my way to school. There was a construction site along the way. For everyone's safety, the construction crew had roped off the sidewalk to keep pedestrians from accidentally falling into a huge hole that had been dug. I crossed the street where work was in progress. Did I see the safety rope? Noooo!

I walked right into the rope, flipped backwards and landed on my back. My head hit the cold, hard concrete with a thud. BAM! I was knocked out again. My parents got paid again. Big money!

Believe it or not, they were paid royally for my misfortune and I never experienced the benefits of a single dime from either of the settlements.

I guess they thought I was too young to understand. Maybe they needed the money for the livelihood of my family. I don't know.

THE CHILD ENTERTAINER

Clearly, due to her own poor education in motherhood, my mom had an earnest, distorted view about the biblical instruction on training up a child in the way she should go. The example she set was hardly beneficial. In fact, it was downright detrimental.

She and I once traveled with my uncle and his son to Myrtle Beach, South Carolina. Mom told me to put on my bathing suit. I thought, for once, the two us would share in some fun, quality time together. It was a beautiful day. My heart soared with joy. What happened next on that day has remained with me to this present time.

"Get on the box, baby," said my uncle. I did as I was told. He was my elder. Mom didn't say a word. Next, he said, "Now dance, baby. Dance and show 'em what you got."

I was ten years old at the time and fully developed with breasts the size of an adult woman. There were grown men all around me—lots of them. I started to dance, seductively, like my uncle coached me to do.

The more seductive I danced the more those men clapped and cheered. I remember the wild look in their eyes. I heard one of them say, "I knew you were gonna be a fine looking' something when you got older. I've been watching you since you were a baby."

Older! I remember thinking they must be crazy. I was a little girl. These were some very strange and sick people I thought.

Deep down, I knew what I was doing was wrong but I couldn't stop. The grownups around me were encouraging it. What was wrong with them? I couldn't stop. What was wrong with me?

My hopes of enjoying the day at the beach with my mom faded. I kept dancing on that soapbox that sad day at Myrtle Beach.

THE DROPOUT

By the time I had reached seventh grade, I had seen and experienced more than the average youth and a great deal more than the normal adult. My relationship with my mother had deteriorated. I resented her. She still drank. She still fought at the drop of a dime. I couldn't understand my dad's silence through it all. And, I was still allowed to run wild in the streets.

Filled with a sense of hopelessness and no encouragement from those who should have cared, I eventually dropped out of junior high school. Uneducated, homeless, gangs, fights, drugs, sex, robbery, prostitution -- all of this became a way of life for me. Much of it stemming from a life of dysfunction. I was broken. No, I was crushed in Spirit. Now when I look back at those days, I am saddened because I didn't know how to change.

At some point, I began to self-mutilate. I became a cutter, which landed me in a mental institution. After ten terrifying months in Washington, D. C.'s Saint Elizabeth Hospital, one day I just walked right out of the facility, undetected. Naturally, I went from the frying pan to the fire. First, I became entangled with a pimp and his wife. After a time of living that awful life, the wife of the pimp came to me one day and said, *"Honey, look, this lifestyle's not for you. Go back to school, get your education. You need to be with your family."* I never saw her again.

My life, which should have taken a positive turn at this point, actually worsened. I couldn't imagine it could until an uncle on my mother's side lured me into a sexual encounter. *"You're fourteen years old, baby,"* he said. *"It's okay. Everybody in the family does it."* Sadly, I believed him. There was some truth to his words. In fact, sometime later I learned that two of my first cousins had married and birthed children together. Surely, there was a family curse that needed to be broken. *"Father, help me to break this curse!"*

STREET LIFE

I wasn't twelve years of age yet but I had already developed a pretty good street hustle. A pimp and his wife, whose names respectively were Jody and Hattie, aided it. The routine went something like this. During the day I would sleep. At nightfall, Jody would send us out to work the streets. Hattie would prepare me for the evening.

First, she would cake my face with foundation, apply a heavy layer of red rouge to my cheeks then line my lips with blood-red lipstick. Hattie and I would then hit the pavement, going from local nightclub to nightclub to earn our keep.

Because I looked much older than my twelve years, I didn't have a problem gaining admission. My size C-cup breasts helped as well. Because I had filled out in all the right places, men on the prowl were easily attracted. Plus, I was young. It was easy--in the beginning.

Hattie and I would sit at the bar all dolled up. After a short while, men would send us drinks. The trick was in not getting too drunk because at some point, we would have clients to service. No one ever suspected that I was a juvenile.

The imprint of that lifestyle made its mark when I became pregnant. It was impossible to know who impregnated me. In the end, I miscarried. Without protection I was also exposing myself to dangerous, deadly disease. I was young.

I was also beaten, raped, shot at and stabbed while I was on the streets. The rape was especially tormenting. I was always in the shower trying to cleanse myself. I couldn't blot out the memory of that attack. Nothing worked and no amount of soap made a difference. To this day, I'm unable to express how dirty I felt. I was too young for this.

The rape became another dark cloud, among many, that followed me everywhere. In fact, hardship and trouble had become closer companions than friends. Where were my parents? I don't know. All I know is that they did not try to locate me.

At some point, I grew tired of the street life. I hated getting in at the break of dawn. I began to despise the touch of strange hands all over me, night-after-night. At a later point, and especially after the rape, I realized the danger. I returned home.

I even returned to school but that didn't last very long. I was still engaging in activity that I shouldn't have. I was young but with an old soul that had been hardened by the streets. I had gotten a taste of the wild life and no amount of discipline could change me at this point. I was pretty much a full-fledged delinquent.

Then, one day, out of the blue, there was a knock at my door. It was Hattie, the pimp's wife. Between the time I had dropped out of elementary school and my ten-month stay at St. Elizabeth's, I had left my schoolbooks behind with Jody and Hattie. My home address was in one of the books.

Hattie didn't say anything at first. She just stood in the doorway. I thought perhaps she was there (at Jody's request) to recruit me back onto the street. Finally, to my surprise she said, "Honey, this lifestyle never was for you. You need to stay in school. Get your education. Stay at home with your family. I'm sorry."

I admit it was good advice but before I could respond, Hattie was heading back towards the elevator in my building. I never had a chance to say anything. She was gone. I never saw Hattie or Jody ever again.

THE UNWANTED IS WANTED!

The streets had ravaged me both physically and mentally. Gangbanging, drinking and drugs, thefts, lying and cheating had become the only life I knew. I was completely out of control. And, I was on the run.

At some point during my life of illegal activity, the law had captured my image. I had become a person of interest to law enforcement. My mug shot was everywhere. There was a wanted poster with my name on it. The cops were hot on my trail. With nowhere to go and exhausted by all the craziness I'd managed to get myself into, I chose to surrender. Yes, I turned myself in to the law.

I clearly remember walking through the doors of that precinct. When they slammed shut behind me, I felt like a prisoner long before the handcuffs were clamped on my wrists. A female officer called me into a meeting room. It was one of those grey, dreary lifeless rooms where criminals are interrogated. I sat and waited. When she finally spoke, she said, "We are going to send you to prison." Her tone was flat, point blank with no emotion. I had committed the crime. It was time to do the time. "Please don't," I begged. My begging didn't help.

It wasn't the first time I had found myself in this position. There was no way out. I was sent to prison. I was given back-to-back sentences, which meant they put all of my time together and sentenced me to twenty-five years behind bars. Good behavior behind bars got me a reduced sentence.

Years later when time grew near for me to be released on parole; I needed to provide a permanent address. I was in my mid-twenties at this point.

The only person I could think of at the time was my mother's sister. I called and asked if I could come live with her until I was able to get a job. To my surprise and relief, she agreed to allow me into her home.

I was officially released from prison on June 17, 1987. I arrived to my aunt's house shortly thereafter to a warm reception. She had prepared a nice room for me. It was a wonderful feeling to be able to put my belongings away in a closet and dresser drawers.

No more jailhouse issue. It was a happy moment for me. I remember thinking to myself that this time I would get it together, live right, do right and stay on the right track. It was a short-lived promise to myself.

After several months of staying with my aunt, a drastic change occurred in her attitude. I couldn't understand why. I respected her property and was staying on the right track. By this time, I still had 180 days to go on parole, which meant I had to have a permanent address for the duration. I hadn't gotten into any trouble and I was following every protocol of a parolee.

Still, my joy was clouded by despair one day when I overheard a telephone conversation between my aunt and my parole officer. At least, I believed it to be my parole officer based on the conversation I overheard. "I want her out of my house," said my aunt. "I'm afraid of her."

What! I couldn't believe my ears. My heart felt as though it'd been struck by a ton of bricks. The sun stopped shining for me on that day. I felt forsaken—again. I met with my parole officer after that.

When he and I sat down to discuss my situation, I stared directly in his eyes and asked, "Where can I go? Who will take me in?" At first, he just sat there, speechless. When he finally opened his mouth to respond, it wasn't what I had expected.

"Your aunt doesn't want you in her home." Okay, so this confirmed that I had been right. It was the two of them speaking a few days earlier. This is messed up, I thought.

I'm also thinking that this guy's deaf or I didn't state my questions clear enough. I asked again. "Who will take me in?" I knew my aunt no longer wanted me in her home. I had overheard her say it from her own mouth on the telephone. All I could do at the moment was stare at my parole officer.

Finally, he said, "Is there someone who can take you in for a while?" At this point, I wanted to scream. I wanted to tell him a lot of things. In truth, my thoughts were not nice. Instead, I remember inhaling deeply, releasing my breath and eventually saying, "No, I do not have anyone who can take me in for a while.

I don't know if it was fate or providence but with no place to call home and no money to pay rent for either an apartment or a room, I was able to look for a job. I eventually found a 'live in' job in rural Virginia. I was employed to provide private nursing services. The pay was great. It was a live-in situation, which meant I had a residence during the remainder of my parole.

I continued providing nursing services in the Virginia household until I found another job that paid more money. I was determined to stay on the right track. I'd lived the hard life long enough. It was time for a new start. I knew in my heart that I had to keep moving forward. I was praying and asking God to help me.

I wanted to earn my G.E.D. while incarcerated, and could have gotten it but the price I had to pay involved sexual favors. It was a price I didn't want to pay. I was tired of being used. I never got my G.E.D.

As time passed, I came across employment ads for cooks in the White House. My heart pumped wild with excitement when I saw this opportunity. Surely, I would be good at this. I applied, thinking I'd be rolling in dough if lucky enough to be hired.

When I arrived for the interview, I was ushered upstairs to the office of the Federal Bureau of Investigations. Hope dimmed. I had a criminal record. There's no way, I thought. After a second thought, I convinced myself not to worry. You were called in for the interview. My heart soared. Everything is going to be okay I reassured myself. I continued to the human resources office.

I was asked to have a seat by my interviewer, a woman who sat tall and erect behind a fancy desk in front of her computer. I could see that her computer screen was lit. "May I have your social security number," she asked. I gave it to her. She keyed in my information, waited a second, frowned and asked, "How did you get in this building?" I panicked. My heart skipped several beats then sank. "M-m-miss," I stuttered.

I took in a deep breath and continued. "Miss, please give me a chance. All I need is to prove myself. You'll see. Please, just give me a chance."

Seconds later, I noticed that she'd lifted her hand from the computer keyboard and dropped it beneath her desk. What I didn't know was that she had depressed some sort of alarm. I was too busy pleading for the job. "Give me a chance, please," I begged. "God has changed me. I'm a new person now. Just give me a chance."

I paused a second and looked her squarely in the eyes. By her look, I could tell she wasn't buying any of what I said. I sensed the situation wasn't going to end pleasantly. I hadn't done anything wrong. All I wanted was a decent job to support myself.

I don't know why but in another second, I adopted the persona of a criminal. I bolted out of her office. By the time security arrived to the meeting room, I had already fled down some stairs and somehow made my way to the main exit.

By the time I reached the busy sidewalk and made my way a little down the street, I looked back to see the agents and police looking down the block after me. For a moment, it felt like I had stepped out of a Hollywood-scripted movie.

As I wandered the streets that day, I felt like someone had taken the sharpest ax and cut me right down the middle, from head to toe. My dreams were shattered. My heart ached. I felt unwanted and of no good use to anyone; especially myself.

Help!
§

Help me, somebody.
I need help.
Help me, somebody.
My home is gone.
I'm all alone.
Help!
Help me, somebody.

With every door of opportunity shutting in my face, it seemed as though everyone hated me. Truly, I felt like a cracked pot shattered into tiny little pieces. What can I do? How can I make it? Where does someone like me find her place in the world?

Times
§

Times I've been alone.
Had no place to call my home.
Walking the streets
day and night,
Satan had me thinking
everything's alright.
Family slammed their doors
in my face.
Hated by every race.
Some would say:
Look-a-there, look-a-there.
Where you goin' girl?
Nowhere!
Smiling faces.
Lying faces.
Dead faces.
So much time,
lost and alone.
That 'ol devil done stole
my mind.

§

*". . . but God has chosen the
foolish things of the world to shame the wise,
and God has chosen the weak things of the
world to shame the things which are strong . .
."*
~ *1 Corinthians 1:27*

The Gang's All Here!

What my family failed to deliver in terms of love and nurturing, joining a gang more than filled that bill. After dropping out of elementary school, being confined in detention centers and mental wards, prostituting, as well as in and out of my parent's home, I upped the ante and joined a local gang.

Being part of a gang made me feel powerful. It made me feel cool and accepted. Finally, I had my crew and somewhere I belonged. No one could touch me without suffering the payback of *our* rage. Regardless of the consequences, we acted as a power of one. I no longer felt alone as a gang member. If there was a problem, I had my gang members to stand with me. We were one.

If I knew then what I know now, maybe I might have understood that I was acting out a need to belong. Gang affiliation and acceptance by its members validated my existence in the world. I wasn't fazed by the potential dangers. I wasn't even fearful of death or imprisonment. I had found a place where I really believed I belonged.

That's all that really mattered at the time. That's all I ever longed for -- to belong.

Anyway, my crew and I would scour the streets in the dark of night, looking and searching for trouble. We would break into people's cars. Without a care, we'd break into homes even while the owners slept. We would take what we wanted and dared the owners to say or do anything, or try to stop us. Yes, we were a gang. We were closer than glue and just as powerful. We were bad and no one dared touch us! Strangely, but more important, I belonged.

I am in no way advocating this lifestyle. Neither am I glamorizing the use of drugs in any form or fashion. This was just a way of life for me, even if stupid. Not only was I a crack smoker, I was a cracked pot. That's why the stuff is dope! We were all dopes, (cracked pots) in need of mending, nurturing and love.

Homelessness

Here is how I journeyed into homelessness. It isn't a pretty picture but it is one that I must share. I figure by shedding light on this journey, perhaps someone, somewhere will be enlightened about what not to do if you want to maintain order in your life. Please believe me when I say even living simply comes with its own set of obstacles and troubles. Drugs only serve to compound the natural course of living.

Anyway, one day I came out of an apartment building after shooting up. I had binged out on drugs to a near overdose. The guy I allowed to help me with the fix injected the dope into my vein too fast. It was potent.

I begged him to stop because I could feel the effects right away. He wouldn't. I snatched the needle out of my arm. In the meantime, my heart raced wildly. The stuff was so pure I could feel my eyelids widening involuntarily. I was lost in a daze. The guy who shot me up simply walked away, leaving me alone in that frenzied state of mind. I almost overdosed.

Somehow I survived that moment. Well,

almost. A week or two went by and one day as I was walking the streets, I started coughing uncontrollably.

At some point, and especially considering the other near fatal overdoses, I should have learned my lesson. I didn't. It is not my intent here to trivialize the good Graces of my Creator but now that I know what I know, I thank God that He looks after babies and fools.

You see, when I couldn't get a fix or high like the one before the last one, I resorted to homemade highs to satisfy my addiction, specifically my alcohol and drug addictions.

Anyway, somewhere down the line, my partner who ran the streets with me suggested that I go into a shelter. Seeing how I ventured into perilous situations so easily, I guess my partner thought a shelter would be best for me. It was just too dangerous living on the streets. I took my partner's advice. When I first arrived to the shelter, the first taste of its reality was like a bitter, numbing pill.

The women's shelter I moved into was populated with bullies and common thugs. They conducted their raggedy lives the same way they'd done on the streets. Nothing was different. They brought the same mentalities into the shelter. There were cliques who would watch my every move. If I went to the restroom, they would rummage through my few belongings. I could tell because my stuff would be in a different place than where I'd left it.

The culprits would eye me like hyenas, ready to devour me in any way possible. Little did they know, I was ready for whatever they had in store. With all the rage and hostility pent up inside of me, I was ready to tear any one of them apart—limb for limb. Shucks! I was a thug too. If they didn't know, they would. I was ready for the challenge. I was a fighter, not a lover. Deep down inside, without saying a word, I silently willed any one of them to come my way. "Please bring it on." They must have understood the fury in my eyes. No one EVER made a move in my direction.

There was little dignity in having absolutely no privacy in a shelter. I thought, when, dear Lord, would I overcome the sadness, depression, despair, confusion and hopelessness.

Believe it or not, I reflected on my mother's words; except, I transposed them to fit my current status. Like my mother had wished, I began to regret that I had ever been born.

Now, by way of experience, I understand why people are reluctant to go into shelters. It is not enough that a person has to guard his/her few meager belongings, the environment is also a sanctioned war zone where a person has to protect her life.

It's sad but the media falls way short when it comes to responsible reporting on the horrid conditions that exist in our city shelters.

I share this because I was subjected to so much of the insanity that exists inside shelter walls. I remember two horrible situations from being a resident of a women's shelter in which one girl was badly beaten while using the bathroom. Another young girl overdosed in the restroom.

These were just two of dozens of horrifying incidents I experienced personally. Sex and sexually transmitted diseases ran rampant inside shelters as well. Life was scary, filthy and dangerous inside those facilities. A roof and walls was all we had. It was hardly a place one could call home.

The one good thing that benefitted me while a resident of the women's shelter was the Outreach Ministry. Different ministries from different churches would come to the shelter to teach the Word of God. At first, I would have no part of it. Over time, I would hear the singing. I always loved to sing. One day, my heart was touched and I decided to join everyone else.

Often, various ministries would pray with us. In other words, we would have church in a most unusual environment. Whenever I found out about the scheduled visits and outreach services, there was an earnest longing within me to get up off my bunk and participate. Something was happening. I didn't know what and I didn't ask. I just went, not knowing what to expect, gain or lose. And, it felt good!

DADDY'S GONE. MOMMA, TOO!

My father was first to pass away. After the injury on his job, momma's stroke and his failing health, he moved back to Texas. At the time of his death, I was a resident of a halfway house [in Texas]. One day, while I waited at a bus stop I happened to run into my stepmother. My father had united with another woman by this time. Because of my predicament, I'd been out of touch with my dad. I asked my stepmother about him. To my surprise, she said he was in the hospital. My rough and tumble personality surfaced. After I had calmed down, both of us traveled to the hospital together to see my dad.

When we arrived, all he asked was, "Where have you been?" I just stared. He looked good but it was difficult to see my dad weak and confined to a hospital bed. He was no longer the tall, strapping figure I remembered as a child. Finally, he said, "It's none of my business, right?" In my heart, I knew he understood my trials. In many ways, I think he saw my troubles in my eyes.

I inched closer to his hospital bed and finally touched him. His legs and feet were as cold as ice. That's when it hit me. Daddy was dying. Sorrow filled my heart. I left the hospital and returned to the halfway house. Before that night was over, I knew my dad had transitioned. A telephone call from my sister confirmed that it was true. "He had made peace with everyone, Mae," she said. When I went to view his body, he did have a peaceful look on his face that seemed to say, "its okay, now, Mae. Don't worry about me. I'm going home." There should have been some comfort in his look but I was mad. Daddy's gone. I'm really alone now, I thought.

When my mother died, I was also unfortunately on lockdown. The day she passed away, I was told to go see the unit manager in the correction facility. Right away, I knew something was wrong. As I made my way to the building, I asked what was going on anyway but didn't receive an answer.

When I arrived to the office, all I said was, "It's my mother, isn't it?" I was told that she had passed away.

"I want to go see her," I said. My unit manager looked me squarely in the eyes and said, "I'll do whatever is necessary to make that happen."

Because I worked in the prison factory, I was earning a small salary. It ended up costing me $460.00 but I got to see my mother. One of the female officers escorted me to South Capitol, the family church. To my surprise, there were so many people there to pay their respects. Believe it or not, my mom had given her life to Christ a few years prior to her death. My rough and tumble, Gin drinking, fist-fighting mother had confessed Jesus Christ as her Savior.
Surely, there was hope for me!

From the church entrance, I could see my mother. Even from that distance, she looked beautiful, at peace and seemed to be resting in God's hands. Suddenly, her life flashed before my eyes as I moved closer to her casket.

After the stroke years ago, my mother had been confined to a nursing home. My aunt, who held power of attorney over her affairs, had placed her there. I was never happy about that but my life was a mess. There was little I could do or say. Sometime later, my mother was also diagnosed with breast cancer. Again, my aunt authorized her surgery.

Momma survived the operation. She even made it back to recovery but died a short while later. I was already filled with anger about my dad's death. Now, I hated my aunt for authorizing my mom's surgery. Finally, I blamed myself for my mom's stroke in the first place. I'm not sure which one was worse. The loss of my parents or the burden of guilt I carried. All I knew for certain was that I felt a great emptiness inside.

I moved closer to my mother's casket. My steps were normal but it felt as though I moved in slow motion. I wanted to cry. I wanted to scream. Finally I was at her casket-side. I leaned in close and kissed my mother's forehead.

From the corner of my eyes, I glimpsed the correction officer watching me. It seemed she understood. Perhaps she wasn't supposed to but I was allowed to stay a little while longer.

I took advantage of the time. While I was there, I had an opportunity to talk too many of my family members. Among them was my baby sister. She looked great. Even though she felt I had abandoned her when my dad sent her away to Texas years ago, I hoped she had come to an understanding that all of that craziness was beyond my control. If I could have done something to make it right, I would have but I was a child, too. What could I have done? I hoped she had buried that dark period of our lives to never be remembered again. I had and I still felt deep love for her.

When it was finally time for me to leave, I said my goodbyes, hugged everyone and wished them well. It was a sad moment but satisfying in so many ways. I left the church with the correction officer at my side. She escorted me into the car and we left.

As I traveled back to prison, I thought of so many things. I really was alone now. The thought of that was frightening. Then I had a bittersweet reminder. As shared before, my mom had given her life to Christ before permanently leaving this earth. Here I was on lockdown, doing time and my mother's soul had been liberated. In a strange kind of way, I was happy.

*"Beloved,
believe not every spirit, but try the spirits
whether they are of God: because many false prophets are gone out
into the world."
~1 John 4:1 (KJV)*

CHURCH: WILL THE REAL CHRISTIANS PLEASE STAND UP!

Hurting people don't realize they hurt until they've been freed from the hurt; that is, no longer feeling the burdensome emotional effects of it. When I was locked in prison, it was a physical lockdown. But there's also a mental lockdown.

What I mean by this is that as human beings, we have a fear of crying out for help. In some cases, it's too much pride. Then, there are those of us who do cry out without reservation. There are people who hear us but are slow to lend a helping hand. Often, there's no help extended at all. Instead, they manufacture gossip about our woes.

Take our church saints for instance. God blesses them but once troubled souls speak truth to addictions and other life battles, it seems as though the saints take flight and run. Some turn against us. One day, they pray for us. The next day, we are cursed by the very same. It seems as if they are offended by the truth.

Worse, personal testimonies are ridiculed and judged. Questions and whispers abound like: She did what? Does she think God is going to forgive her for what she did? How could she say such things? Why would she tell her business like that?

Yes, dear readers, these are our super, duper saints in the church. And, now, their judgmental attitudes have ushered us right back where we started—out of the church and back on the streets! These attitudes can cause new believers to shrink from church attendance. It can cause serious trust issues as well.

If Jesus Christ, our Lord and Savior made himself a small thing just to save us, who is greater than He that they should look down on a person? Absolutely no one!

There, I said it. No one should be looking down on another. I have encountered many church folk who do, however. "Girl, what is that she's wearing?" How unreasonable is this sentiment when it is not what's on the outside that matters but the condition of the heart that counts.

I've known many people who decided to give their lives to Christ but didn't because of the steely-eyed, judgmental looks of long-time members of the church. It doesn't make good Christian sense. Jesus didn't come to judge. He came to save.

Likewise, people don't come to church after a life on the streets or after being hurt almost beyond repair by family, friends and even enemies, to be judged. They come seeking healing. They come hoping to start fresh. They come hoping to understand the Salvation they've heard others talk about.

Where there is the absence of grace, mercy and acceptance by long-time churchgoers, many new believers are drawn back to the streets, drugs, homelessness, despair and many other vices; all of which leads to spirit and soul deterioration.

Young girls, lost and lonely in the world, are swept away by the charming advances of men who show any signs of caring. Of course, we know this is the trickery of sheep in wolves clothing. Ultimately, it's all about sex or pimping a lost soul out to the streets. I know because I've been that young girl.

There are hundreds of thousands of others at the same fork in the road right now. We, as Christians, need to cease indicting the poorly dressed and different looking new believers who enter our gates, and begin to do more accepting.

Will the real Christians please stand up?

There was this one woman from a church I attended who took me into her home to help with her housecleaning. She had a long list of rules like: Don't eat this. Don't eat that. Don't do this and on and on. On the other hand, she dumped all of her mental garbage in my lap. Had I become a magnet to bad luck, bad people?

Another time, a woman opened up her home to me until I was fully back on my feet. She was from another church I once attended. At first, I thought this was the opportunity of a lifetime. I thought someone was finally looking beyond my faults. Finally, someone saw my abilities. And, finally, I accepted her offer and eventually moved into her home. She did help me secure a job but as time passed, things began to sour.

Out of the blue, she began to insist that I needed to purchase my own groceries even though she had a fully stocked kitchen. To add insult to injury, she would prepare lavish meals but never offered a single morsel to me. More amazing, she would walk around the house, cussing and fussing me for no apparent reason. One day, she threatened to have her son inflict bodily harm. What! If her son had laid a hand on me, little did she know, I could and would fight. Snap! Snap! I'd been fighting all my life. I was no stranger to battle. Thankfully, I never had to come to blows with either of them.

Her verbal abuse and threats did not compare to her bug-infested home. There were roaches, trillions of them that crawled from the woodwork. I couldn't open a bag of chips without being attacked by them. No amount of bug spray helped.

As awful as it was to continue living there, I had to remain. There was nowhere else for me to go. I didn't want to return to the streets. I'd had my fill of the shelters. And, I certainly didn't want to do anything to land me in prison again. I had nowhere else to go.

IF I CAN'T FIND HELP IN THE CHURCH THEN WHERE?

I was released from prison on June 17, 1987. I tried re-connecting with former church members but things weren't the same. Finding a place to fit in was becoming more and more difficult. Many of the leaders talked a good talk but that was about all it was—talks! I'll share more on that later.

Leading up to that point as I was trying to settle into a new life, I remember sitting under the voice of this one Pastor. Suddenly, something stirred inside of me. I felt a strong pull to rise from the pew, go up to the altar and give my life to Christ. I really wanted to give my life to God. I wanted to feel free. I wanted that love and peace that the Pastor was preaching about.

However, there was another spirit warring with my flesh. That spirit was the street life I had known for so long. There's something about that street life that I just could not shake. In the end, I took the walk up to the altar that day but I wasn't committed. Unfortunately, I strayed again.

Times before this, I attended other churches but eventually I left because after telling my story as the Lord lead me to do, everyone started looking at me as though I had some kind of contagious disease. They didn't want me around. I guess they couldn't handle the truth.

There were evangelists, missionaries and even Pastors who recognized me from my prison days. They had seen me before my release and knew I had no place to go. They knew full well that I was living on the streets. I even asked a few of them for help. Like I shared earlier, they talked a good talk but that was about all -- talk. Rarely did anyone keep a single promise to help me in my time of need.

There was one Pastor though, a woman, who would come and get me and take me to her home. She was acquainted with some of my story and suggested that I write it all down. She suggested that I publish it in the church newsletter. Thinking it was a good idea, I agreed. However, once I began to provide my story in full, she began to condemn me. I ceased from telling her anything further. Later, I learned she was just a busybody who wanted to inch her way into my personal business for reasons I'll never understand. In my innocence, I thought she wanted to help. And, yes, this was a Pastor!

Trust issues and anger all came back in a rush. How could this woman stand in the pulpit and betray one's trust at the same time? Was truth anywhere in her soul? Where was the love she professed? I was furious and knew I had to distance myself from this false prophet. I started church hopping. I wanted to fit in someplace but I didn't know where. There were cracked pots—smiling faces, lying tongues—everywhere.

Another time, this woman from church offered work. She wanted me to clean and maintain her home. The only problem with this was she wanted me to perform these services without pay! Clearly, that didn't work out for me. Why was I drawn to people who wanted to control and use me I thought? Slave labor had long been abolished. Why was everyone trying to shackle me? I had done my time behind bars. I had paid the price for wrongdoing. All I wanted was to be accepted at this point.

My life unfolded the way it did to testify of God's Glory; but some churches didn't even want me to open my mouth about my victories. "Just don't say anything about being in prison," they said. "You don't have to tell everything." God have mercy on them!

> ***"When you come to Christ, you were circumcised; but not by a physical procedure. Christ performed a spiritual circumcision—the cutting away of your sinful nature. ~ Colossians 2:11***

On another occasion, after I shared my story before a church congregation, many of the members stopped associating with me. I thought perhaps I had a plague or something.

Was there a fit for me anywhere? As much as I hate to admit it, at this point I was beginning to dislike pastors and church folk alike. Snobbish looks, snide remarks and stink attitudes were hardly what I considered as a Christian lifestyle. I didn't know where to go or turn.

I couldn't believe this was happening with church folk. I couldn't believe the one place where I should have been healed was hurting me in more ways than I could number.

During those moments of despair, all I could

think about was returning to prison. I even considered ways to return. At least, behind bars, there was a community in which I could relate. Inmates, in many ways, were like family. I knew what they did and how they acted. Behind bars, there was only one name given to all—convict. Neither guilt nor innocence mattered. All that mattered if one is incarcerated is that we're all convicts. That never changed. All I wanted beyond those prison walls was to be part of a Christian family who acted like Christians, who held firm to that name in character and love, and changed not.

CONVERSION

I did believe in my heart and eventually confessed Jesus as my Lord and Savior, according to God's Word in Romans 10:9:

"Confess with your mouth that Jesus is Lord . . ."

Funny, when this happens the real battle begins. The enemy is mad and at war to keep us off the road to recovery. My battle began in the mind. I started wondering how and why I had come to this point of conversion. I questioned whether the Lord was walking with me. I began to doubt my abilities and myself. I felt unstable. That's when Colossians 2:11 came to mind.

AM I WORTHY OF SALVATION?

I often wondered if I was worthy of salvation. Could God really use a person like me? Could He use a person with a past like mine?

Some churches I visited preached that murderers and evildoers were destined for hell. Some even preached that they didn't believe God was able to forgive? Hogwash!

There are many biblical instances where God forgave murderers, adulterers, and even whoremongers. If He did it centuries ago, surely I could be forgiven centuries later, especially after I confessed my sins and repented of them.

In fact, if my God was not a forgiving God, how did Abraham (a liar), Moses (a murderer), Jacob (a trickster), David (an adulterer), Solomon (lustful of women), make it to Faith's Hall of Fame? Hebrews 11 tells of these and many more individuals who were flawed and while not fully aware of the promise of our Savior, remained and lived a life faithful in the Lord. If God was not a forgiving God, what need is there for Jesus Christ? Because of Jesus and our confession of Him, we are indeed forgiven. Never again will I believe the lies. I know God forgives. In fact, I am living proof. When I was younger I didn't have either a proper understanding or the ability to grasp the positive things that were said to me about who I could be in this life.

But now, after experiencing what I experienced, knowing what I know, I understand what some of the elders in my life meant when they said long ago that, "God has a calling on your life."

It would take a long time and many more life-threatening experiences in the pit of hell before I realized this, however. Truth is, at some point, I'd lost all ability to feel natural, human emotions.

The only feeling I'd grown accustomed to was despair. I was miserable so I hurt others. I could no longer love. In fact, all I saw in my immediate future was my own death.

Everything was closing in on me. There was no one to whom I could talk. Momma and daddy were gone. I didn't have anyone to love even if they had issues of their own.

There was no one to give me a single, reassuring hug. All I needed was someone in my life to tell me everything would be just fine. If only someone had told me I could make it, be someone great, what would my life have been like?

Curse, Unknown

> *"Had I known what I know now,*
> *I would have tried to break the pattern of pain*
> *that had*
> *infected my family's behavior.*
> *As it was, I was young, vulnerable and*
> *just as infected as the rest.*
> *It was a particular hell on earth.*

Like I said, at the height of my despair, I prayed to God to just let me die. That's how intense it was at the time. Obviously, it wasn't God's Will that I should die during those dark hours.

Nevertheless, little did I know that He would take me through several more stages to sharpen my character, establish a good temperament, as well as prepare me as a living witness to His Glory.

My mistake was telling others. My family, who were dream assassins, took my hope and aspirations, chewed them up and spat them out for the dogs.

What I mean by this is that my relatives found it easier to put a negative spin on anything positive. They couldn't accept greatness in others without expressing the weakness in themselves. Truly, they were cracked pots.

For instance, when I was growing up around them, all I ever heard them say about me were things like: "You are no good. You are a bad seed. You need to be locked up in a mental hospital and kept there." Well, I pretty much lived up to my family's every wish (and curse).

Looking back, I came to realize that they must have been incredibly miserable themselves to want to crush my dreams? Or any dream for that matter. One time, my mom and her people went so far as to say, "You are not my child. I hate you Mae."

I prayed: Dear Lord in Heaven, how can I learn to love after being exposed to this kind of poison?

Soon, and very soon, God started to answer.

Let brotherly love continue.
Be not forgetful to entertain
strangers: for thereby some have

*entertained angels unawares.
Remember them that are in bonds,
as bound with them;
and them which suffer adversity,
as being yourselves
also in the body.
~Hebrews 13:1,
(KJV)*

MY EARTH ANGEL: MOMMA DAVIS

While I was serving my prison sentence, I met one of the most incredible individuals I have ever known. In fact, she was the closest thing to a true mother figure I had ever experienced.

I called her Momma Davis. She was a member of her church's social justice ministry. She would come to the prison on behalf of her church to speak with the inmates. Her mission was to share the message of the Good News of Jesus.

After several visits, she and I developed a wonderful relationship. We would talk about a lot of things. The more we talked the more I grew to love and appreciate her. She gave me hope. Her words of encouragement really helped to strengthen me.

Once I was released from prison, I remembered those meaningful, heartfelt conversations I had been blessed to have with Momma Davis. That's how deeply she affected me. I decided to try and locate her. I wasn't sure if this was a good idea or not but I continued with my search anyway.

Once I found out where she lived, I grew a little nervous. I wasn't sure how she would react to my coming to her home. In fact, I almost decided against it. I'm not sure what or why I dismissed those thoughts but I did. I went to Momma Davis' home.

Momma Davis had her own thoughts. She was strong and gentle at the same time. I think that's what impressed me the most. She had compassion on me and knew her heart was guiding her along the right path. She allowed me to move in with her. Often, she prayed for me, saying she saw how the Lord had taken the scales from my eyes.

Acts 9:18: "Instantly something like scales fell from Saul's eyes and he regained his sight. Then he got up and was baptized."

Once I was settled in her home, Momma Davis would come to the room she'd prepared for me. She would knock first and say, "Mae, can I come in?" I wasn't accustomed to that. I'd been told when to eat, when to go to the restroom, when to play and when to sleep. This was a courtesy that shocked me.

I would open the door and Momma Davis would say, "Mae, honey, you are free in my house. You can keep the door open. Above all, you do not have to hide food in your room. That's why I have a kitchen."

I didn't know how to accept this either. My level of trust was still at an all-time low. For so long I had been watching out for myself. The invisible wall I had built was tall and strong. Momma Davis crushed all of this with her kindness and understanding.

Momma Davis was the closest I have ever come to experiencing an earth angel, and God blessed me to experience her generous, caring nature for thirty glorious years. She has since transitioned to glory and I had the privilege of attending her home going service. Her Spirit lives on for me and I will be forever thankful to God for placing her in my life. She was a wonderful, kind-hearted woman who influenced my life greatly. She made me want to live and live right to the best of my ability. I pray Momma Davis' soul rests in paradise in the presence of the Lord, our God!

A CALL TO EVANGELIZE

I took a month's vacation from everything. It was actually more like a sabbatical, if you will, so that I might travel to Texas. I was on a mission from God. I had family in Texas that I hadn't seen in years. God had spoken to me about family matters and what I should do, say and pray about.

After coordinating my trip and contacting reliable family members to help with transportation, everything had begun to fall into place. Between my husband and a dear cousin, I was able to be on my way to Texas. God will always work it out!

For the duration of my trip to Dallas, Texas I met so many hurting people. It started with a white woman who sat next me. After introducing herself, she went on to tell me about her dying mother and husband who suffered with Hepatitis. We prayed right there on the bus. That was the start of many intimate confessions that were shared by hurting people.

From Mississippi to Louisiana, I prayed for each one. I prayed for people torn from their families. I prayed with individuals who were clearly emotionally disturbed. When those who confessed their broken hearts for one reason or another, I prayed with them, too.

Almost two days later of traveling, meeting and praying with perfect strangers, I arrived to Dallas, Texas. Just as I had been told, my nephew was waiting at the bus depot to transport me to his home. For my visit, he and his wife had prepared the most wonderful accommodations in their beautiful home. I can't begin to tell you how glad my heart was to see them doing so well. I felt pure joy from the very beginning.

Once I had greeted everyone, reminisced a little about the good old times, I decided to shed my weary travel clothes and freshen up. It had been a very long trip.

I thought I would take a quick nap that turned into overnight slumber. I remember laying my head on the pillow but can't recall anything after that. I fell asleep faster than lightning. And, oh my, did I sleep! It was peaceful sleep.

All in all, everything was shaping up beautifully. I was overjoyed to have followed the calling. It was sweet justice!

When there is genuine trust in Almighty God, He will bring about justice. For it is written in Isaiah 61:7:

"Instead of shame and dishonor, you will enjoy a double share of honor. You will possess a double portion of prosperity in your land, and everlasting joy will be yours."

I have learned that wherever a person is in life (emotionally, professionally or otherwise) there are more blessings ahead than behind. I've learned to enjoy my days fully as I wait on God's almighty form of justice.

DEATH PAIN

Before I could become victor rather than victim, I had to overcome what I have termed *death pain*. What I mean by this is that I felt damaged and useless with all the disorder in my life. The best definition I can provide for *death pain* is emotional and physical distress dragged into adulthood from infanthood. It is the stuff that builds up in the body like toxic waste and slowly destroys mind, body and soul. It is a poison. The dysfunction of *death pain* nearly destroyed me.

Oh, what a glorious day it was when I read Psalm 46:1: *"God is our refuge and strength and ready to help in times of trouble."*

With a sincere cry for help to God, the solutions started to manifest themselves. I didn't know it at the time but as I grew in the Word, I came to understand that God had always been by my side, waiting for me to put my 'death pain' in His hands. On my own, I couldn't do it. As many times as I tried to do it my way, I failed. After failing so many times, I wanted to throw in the towel and give up completely. In truth, I really wanted to die. But God, in His perfect wisdom, had something else in store for me. I can truthfully confess that He was there as I moved through the valley of death.

He is available to everyone, no matter the creed, color, condition or crisis. All it takes is the earnest desire and a sincere heart.

"For He has rescued us from the kingdom of darkness and transformed us into the kingdom of his dearest Son." ~ Colossians 1:13

You Were Always With Me!
§

*You could have left me
standing there, all alone,
with no one,
no one to care.
You promised me
You'd be on time;
and, you did just what you said.
O, friend of mine.
That's when you
blessed me.
That's when you
blessed me.
That's when you
blessed me.
You did just what
you said.*

A VERY SPECIAL GIFT FROM GOD

My beloved, my honey, Nazareth, who eventually became my hubby, entered my life during my transformation to a spirit-filled lifestyle from the dark and dangerous life I once lived. My childhood dream of long ago was finally fulfilled. Not by my might but God's. It happened at the point when I was still in and out of women's shelters. It's amazing how God provides our needs in His time rather than in the time of our personal wants. When Nazareth and I first met, we realized we were meant to be together. We talked a lot. After some time had passed and we'd gotten to know all about one another, we began to encourage one another's hopes and dreams. That's how a healthy relationship should develop. Far too often, relationships are rushed into based on the physical when it should be about the inward, spiritual strength. Anyway, from the very beginning, my husband accepted me just as I was. He was loving, supportive and encouraging. of everything I did. He was never judgmental about my past or present. It seemed like he had been placed in my life for a specific reason. I say this because we realized our compatibilities right away. Once we became friends, everything else about our relationship fell into place.

Sometime later, we both agreed that our meeting was providential. We accepted that God's hand was definitely at work in our meeting. Since we were both in agreement and on one accord, we began planning out our lives. After eight years of courtship, we decided to finally marry. I am happy to share that we have celebrated this union for twelve wonderful years. Aside from my mentor, Momma Davis, and HEALING FROM DELIVERANCE MINISTRY

How Great Thou Art!

On a Tuesday, back on August 20, 2013, I arrived to my doctor's office for a routine physical only to be rushed to emergency. That same day, I was placed in intensive care. Days later, I nearly died.

"How are you feeling today," asked my doctor. She went through her regular routine of checking off something in my folder. I waited until she had finished writing.

"Not too good," I said. I suffered from Chronic Obstructive Pulmonary Disease (COPD). Because of that I hadn't been feeling my normal best for most of the morning but I didn't think it was anything too serious. My husband was at work so I made my way to the hospital alone.

"Okay, let's check your vitals," said my doctor. She probed here and there then proceeded to check my heart rate, lungs and blood pressure.

All of a sudden, I couldn't stop coughing. It was nonstop. A wave of nausea overwhelmed me. My doctor called for emergency. A nurse arrived with a wheelchair seconds later. My breathing was labored and the nausea continued. Once in emergency, I was hooked up to oxygen and closely monitored. Meantime, my husband was contacted at work. He left work immediately and rushed to the hospital. After speaking with the doctors about my condition, he was told I had to remain in the hospital.

Eventually, I was moved to a regular room where an IV, oxygen pump and pressure cuffs were hooked up. All kinds of monitoring devices were hooked to almost every inch of my body.

Somewhere, the saints were praying for me.

My Pastor told me so when she telephoned. In fact, she said a prayer vigil had begun as soon as news spread that I had been hospitalized. Part of my healing was in knowing others thought enough of me to pray for me.

A short while later, another Pastor and her husband came to visit. I was still in intensive

care but was now able to eat. As I was eating, a crushing pain in the center of my chest nearly took my breath away. Monitors beeped. "It hurts," I screamed.
"It hurts so badly. Please stop the pain." It felt like a heart attack.

Doctors and nurses rushed to my bedside. They moved fast, trying to save my life. With all the excitement going on around me I can't explain why I chose that moment to glance out the hospital window. All I remember is that when I did, I saw this big cloud with mid-sized clouds beneath it. They looked like steps. Doctors and nurses were working frantically. I looked out the window again. This time, I saw this brilliant white light. I was drawn to it. I remember smiling. I also recall singing *"How Great Thou Art"*. The next thing I knew, my doctor was telling me I needed to rest. "Close your eyes," he said. "You're going to be just fine." he was right. I was in intensive care for 3 days and then moved back to a regular room.

I truly believe God allowed me to cross over for a glimpse of the other side, if you will. It was a foretaste of things to come. What reassurance! My time in the hospital was to heal but as it turned out, I was there to share the Good News of Jesus Christ also. People I didn't know began coming to my room, pouring out their hearts to me. So many of them share so much about their lives. Some just wanted prayer. Others desired to find a church home. I became God's mouthpiece.

Surely, God was preparing me for the people he would send my way in the days and years to come. Oh yes, *"How Great Thou art"*.

Healing From the Heart Deliverance Ministries

After years of drugs and alcohol abuse and now COPD, my health was now under attack. Yes, I had survived the wild life but it was time to pay the price for my carelessness. I was now in and out of the hospital.

Another time while I waited to see my doctor, I looked around the waiting room. It was filled with people from wall-to-wall. Each one of them suffered from some physical ailment. Since it is my nature to talk, I struck up conversations with many of them. I came to learn that some had terminal illnesses while others were there to be treated for less threatening conditions. So much hurt. So much pain. I wondered what these people had suffered in life. I wondered if any had been like me -- shattered and shunned -- a cracked pot.

I left my doctor's office that day and boarded the city bus. As we moved from stop to stop, I listened to surrounding conversations. It was as if I had been blessed with a keener sense of hearing. There was one woman who declined her friend's invitation to go drinking. I overheard her say that she had been diagnosed with Sclerosis of the liver. Another time, while waiting at the bus stop, a young man approached me and openly confessed his drug addiction. For some reason, people just started talking to me, telling me about their problems and hardships.

They were sad, lonely individuals who needed someone to listen. I could relate. I knew firsthand what it felt like to exist yet be invisible at the same time. I knew what it felt like to scream for *help* and have my cries fall on deaf ears. That's when I began to realize my purpose in life. For every problem I faced early on, there was a purpose in each. I needed to teach by example and experience. I needed to testify of God's goodness.

On May 2, 2013 around 7:30 a.m., God spoke to me about all of this. I put two and two together and concluded that I must work for You, Lord. I've been at death's door on far too many occasions but you kept me. I realized that I could not be ashamed to share the Good News of Jesus Christ with anyone. His Grace is sufficient.

Here I am, I thought. I'm open to whatever it is you want me to do or say, Lord. I will go wherever I must go. I will speak to whoever will hear and receive the Good News!

That's how and when HEALING FROM THE HEART DELIVERANCE MINISTRIES came about. It is a ministry that keeps me praying for everyone. I evangelize everywhere God sends me. I don't preach to people. I listen.

Sometimes I'm moved to give a much-needed hug or caress someone's hand. HEALING FROM THE HEART DELIVERANCE MINISTRIES is designed to lift the spirits of the depressed, sick and lost. Its purpose is to help those who are broken emotionally, physically and spiritually. It is not about me. It is all about Jesus!

I Owe It All
§

Oh, Lord, I love you today.
You made my blind eyes see.
Open doors so wide for me
Enemies made low
giving me victory.
I owe it all to you.
To you, Lord,
I owe it all to You.

For lost souls like you and me
Jesus died on Calvary.
Wallowing in sin,
Jesus took me right on in.
A new joy I found,
A new peace within
Perfect peace now abounds.
I owe it all to You.
To You, Lord,
I owe it all to You.
Oh, yes, Lord . . . I do!

NO MORE SCALES: I CAN SEE CLEARLY NOW!

It's a new day for me now. I'm headed in a new direction. My sight has been restored. I can clearly see God's plans for me. Just like the Israelites, I am following the cloud. I have learned that age doesn't matter to God. He will use anyone who is a willing vessel to accomplish His work.

At last, I am able to claim the inheritance that God promised His child. It is by Faith that I'm looking forward to new heights, conquering new territories, and whatever else God has in store for me. He has brought me from a mighty long way. My wilderness was the test and by His strength and love, I made it through. I believe He has plans to take me to even greater heights.

In many ways, I have the Faith of Caleb who, at 85 years of age, asked and received his inheritance. After forty years in the wilderness, surviving the battlefields of death, he boldly asked for what had been promised: *"Now then, just as the LORD promised, he has kept me alive for ten years since the time he said this to Moses, while Israel moved about in the wilderness. So here I am today, in my seventies! I am still as strong today as the day Moses sent me out; I'm just as vigorous to go out to battle now as I was then. Now give me this hill country that the LORD promised me that day. You yourself heard then that the Anakites were there and their cities were large and fortified, but, the LORD helping me, I will drive them out just as he said."* (Joshua 14:6-12, NIV)The Anakites in my life were drugs, alcohol and that awful season on the streets. But the Lord's compassion and strength enabled me to win the battle over those things.

God has brought a great reward in my life in recompense for the abuse I suffered in my personal wilderness. Although many winters have passed, I have a wonderful life. He has blessed me. He's working everything out for me as I work to do His Will. My age does not matter.

A NEW DAY

Oh, it's a brand new day.
Yes, Lord, in every way.
Oh, it's a brand new day.
No more worries.
Oh, no, no, no.
It's a brand new day.
Sorrows, no more.
Jesus took me off the streets.
He set this captive free.
Oh, yes He did ya'll.
Oh, yes He did.
It's a brand new day.
And, I'm loving the Lord for
this new me.
Out of the garbage cans and
cardboard boxes,
my body for food
mental toxins.
Rapings ceased and beatings, too.
Old things behind
a life brand new.
Oh, it's a brand new day.
Yes, Lord, in every way.
No more worries.
Oh, no, no, no.
It's a brand new day.
sorro

A REVELATION: MY CALL TO MINISTER

I am not a mistake. I was not an accident. I do have a purpose. Satan thought he had me. He thought he would take me out. God said, "Not so." God always restores what's lost. God takes care of those He calls His own. All we need to do is trust Him. *"I will give you back what you lost to the swarming locusts, the hopping locusts, the stripping locusts, and the cutting locusts. It was I who sent this great destroying army against you. Once again, you will have all the food you want, and you will praise the Lord, your God who does these miracles for you. Never again will my people be disgraced."* (Joel 2:25-26)

I never did fit in, not even when I was drawn into the world's system of drugs and alcohol. I stood out like a sore thumb even then. You see, I was already set apart. Sadly, I just didn't know it at the time.

When God called me, I had no money. I had no place to call home. There was no food to nourish my broken body. My shoes were worn through the soles. I walked around suffering with cracked, bleeding feet. When I heard God's call, I had nothing.

In many ways, I was the prodigal daughter. God didn't leave me. I had abandoned Him. He was always there, drawing me nearer and nearer to Him. In fact, when God calls, nothing and no one can hold us back. I have been given a new beginning to make a difference in the lives of others. Sure, there are hustlers, gangbangers, murderers and thieves but God, the great deliverer, can change these individuals too. Don't consider yourselves so holy because you never smoked, drank or lusted. We are all cracked pots in need of mending.

All of God's work is marvelous and His best work is very often evident in the fallen, downtrodden and forgotten souls. Show me someone who cannot read and God will become the Master teacher. Someone who can't speak and God will give you a platform from which you can tell the world of his Grace and Mercy.

YOU WERE THERE ALL THE TIME

You were there all the time.
You, Lord, were there all the time.
Thank You, Lord, for being there.
I was happy, thank you.
You fed me, thank you.
When I thirst, you gave me drink.
Thank you.
You, Lord, were there all the time.
I was homeless, you gave me shelter.
Thank you.
Feet bare and crusted, You provided shoes.
Thank You.
Tattered and naked, you provided clothing.
Thank You.
You, Lord, were there all the time.
When I was in prison, You visited me.
Oh, yes, You were there all the time.
Yes, Lord, You were there all the time.

*Elder Mae is a
member of Kingdom Refuge Ministries
International
as well as Founder of
HEALING FROM THE HEART DELIVERANCE
MINISTRIES.*

*AS A prayer warrior, Minister Fogle's
life's mission is to help hurting individuals.*

Free!
§

Lord, I go where You want me to go
I say what You want me to say.
I'll be what You want me to be.
O Lord, yes, uses me.

Lord, I will walk where You want me to walk.
I will say to Your people,
"How You have set the captives free."
Just look at me.
Lord, You have said in Your Word,
"Who is free, is free indeed."
Thank You, Lord, for setting me free.

PSALM 30 ~ KJV

I will extol thee, O Lord;
for thou hast lifted me up,
and hast not made my foes to rejoice over
me.

O Lord my God, I cried unto thee, and
thou hast healed me.

O Lord, thou hast brought up my soul from
the grave:
thou hast kept me alive, that I should not
go down to the pit.

Sing unto the Lord, O ye saints of his,
and give thanks at the remembrance of his
holiness.

For his anger endureth but a moment; in
his favour is life:
weeping may endure for a night, but joy
cometh in the morning.

And in my prosperity I said, I shall never

*be moved.
Lord, by thy favour
thou hast made my
mountain to stand
strong:
thou didst hide thy
face, and I was
troubled.
I cried to thee, O
Lord; and unto the
Lord I made
supplication.*

*What profit is there in my blood, when I go
down to the pit?
Shall the dust praise thee? shall it declare
thy truth?*

*Hear, O Lord, and have mercy upon me:
Lord, be thou my helper.*

Thou hast turned for me my mourning into dancing:
thou hast put off my sackcloth, and girded me with gladness;
to the end that my glory may sing praise to thee,
and not be silent. O Lord my God,
I will give thanks unto thee forever.
Amen!

For speaking engagements, consultation or special prayer, please contact the author, Elder Mae Fogle at:
202-569-5426

§

"Then he [Jesus] told them many things in parables, saying: "A farmer went out to sow his seed. As he was scattering the seed, some fell along the path, and the birds came and ate it up. Some fell on rocky places, where it did not have much soil. It sprang up quickly, because the soil was shallow. But when the sun came up, the plants were scorched, and they withered because they had no root. Other seed fell among thorns, which grew up and choked the plants. Still other seed fell on good soil, where it produced a crop—a hundred, sixty or thirty times what was sown. Whoever has ears, let them hear."

Matthew 13:3-9, (NIV)

"It is our heartfelt prayer that everyone experiences the peace of God, the joy of his love and the prosperity of his bountiful blessings."
Nazareth and Elder Mae Fogle

Whenever feelings of abandonment, sorrow, worthlessness, helplessness, sadness, or any emotion common to man overwhelms, search these Scriptures at the onset and allow the Word of God to fill your hearts. Wait on God. Trust God and experience the transformation that is only possible with Him.

◊

I am more than a conqueror. ~ Romans 8:37

I am a child of God. ~ Romans 8:16

I have a citizenship in heaven. ~ Ephesians 2:19

I have been blessed with all spiritual blessings. ~ Ephesians 1:3

I belong to Christ. ~1 Corinthians 7:22

I am healed because he took my infirmities and bore my sicknesses. ~ Matthew 8:17

I am a new creature in Christ. ~ Corinthians 5:17

I will keep you in perfect peace whose mind is stayed on the Lord.
~ Isaiah 26:3

"The Lord is my strength and my defense; he has become my salvation."
~ Exodus 15:2

"My Spirit, who is on you, will not depart from you." ~ Isaiah 59:21

"For I am convinced that neither death nor life, neither angels nor demons, neither the present nor the future, nor any powers, neither height nor depth, nor anything else in all creation, will be able to separate us from the love of God that is in Christ Jesus our Lord."
~ Romans 8:38-39

Following are some valuable resources for those who would like to begin the healing journey.

www.nlm.nih.gov/medilineplus/hepatitisc.html

www.uptodate.com/contents/hepatitis-c-beyond-the-basics

www.liverfoundation.org

Center for Disease Control and Prevention (CDC):
1-800-232-4636

www.addictioncareoptions.com
This website is associated with the:
The National Alcoholism and Substance Abuse Information Center (NASAIC) that maintains a continuously updated
national database of alcohol treatment centers.

www.therefuge-ahealingplace.com
(ptsd-treatment and child-sexual-abuse)
Learn about treating child and adolescent sexual abuse trauma. The Refuge is a Post-Traumatic Stress Disorder treatment center focused on trauma rehab and co-occurring addictions.
Telephone: 1-855-338-3048

Epilogue

I have shared these experiences and events because there are so many hurting people from all walks of life. Rarely is it publicized but I believe some of our teachers and leaders who are in revered positions, including bishops, pastors, ministers, evangelists and deacons, are also victims of some type of hurt.

While any misconduct or violation of their person is no fault of their own, I believe many individuals have chosen to remain silent out of some unfounded fear or imagined shame.

There is no shame in admitting the truth. The shame rests in silence. The shame rests in pent up anger that will not allow hurting individuals to find peace in their hearts and minds. The shame rests in what might be lost like church membership or the love of a spouse or the judgment of friends and family. The gains of purging heart and mind of pain are far greater than anything that might be lost.

"Then Jesus said, "Come to me, all of you who are weary and carry heavy burdens, and I will give you rest." This, alone, teaches us that God is our helper!

When we confess our sins and repent and pray for others, and look to Jesus Christ who is Lord, He will heal our bruises, restore our brokenness, and peel away un-forgiveness— layer-by-layer. He did it for me. He will do it for hurting people everywhere.

I was hurting and thought alcohol would cure my internal pain. When that didn't work, I advanced to marijuana. After growing weary of that, I turned to cocaine (in all available forms). In times of a needy "fix" and lack of finances, I resorted to homemade remedies.

These were low points in my life and desperate people do desperate things. In my blindness, I honestly admit that I didn't know any better. The end result of exposing my body to these deadly concoctions resulted in Hepatitis C, COPD and many other health issues.

My flesh loved what I once fed it and now I must pay in the flesh. Nevertheless, I continue to hold onto God's unchanging promises. That's all I encourage anyone to do. That's all anyone can do. Allow the Lord to come into your life, right now. Confess Romans 10:9-10. Confess and mean it with all of your heart. Even though the Blood of the Lamb saves me, I learned from experience that when one indulges without regards for health, eventually there is a price to pay. That has not stopped me from praying God's strength in every health trial.

I've been so sick and tired of my wayward life that I've wanted to die. I even fled to Texas once to be with my big sister. She was the only one who could talk to me and I'd listen. She had a warm and soothing Spirit that could make me stop whatever I was doing. That is, until I found my way around town. Once that happened, I returned to my old tricks -- drinking, drugs and the dangerous streets. I even sang with a local band for a while until I made the mistake of eyeing one of the band members. My sister tried to help me but she knew I had to want to help myself first. Prison was supposed to rehabilitate me. It didn't. I was an addict. Addicts are strange and confused beings. I even thought a man of wealth could help only to learn their wealth was a means to keep me shackled to my addictions.

One nearly caused me to lose my sight from a blow to the head with a soda bottle. He was wealthy, sneaky and mean. An attempt to seek revenge could have potentially landed me in jail again. I allowed another hustler to add me to his stable of women. I didn't care. My reward was drugs. I couldn't help myself. My addiction was a cover for a deeper issue -- emotional pain!

At some point, I remembered a promise that I once made to myself. That promise was that I would never be like my mother; except, I had become just like her in every imaginable way. In some ways, I was worse.

No matter the storm, heartache, feelings of rejection or loneliness, continue to acknowledge the Lord in every situation and believe His promise to bring us through them all if we simply trust Him. Give God a chance and experience His blessed goodness. Experience His marvelous love.

Pray God's strength in every situation. Trust him. Understand that it isn't human might but divine might that can transform trouble into triumph and trials into testimonies. Lean not to your own understanding.

I've learned to ask God to order my steps. That's all you have to do, too! Ask Him to place you in a church that rightly divides the Word of God. Sit under God's Word with the expectation of hearing clearly in order to experience healing of the mind, spirit and soul. God can make a change. Nothing, I mean absolutely nothing, is impossible for God.

There is no situation too large or small for Him. He will do exactly what He said. He is not a man that He should lie. Trust Him! Meditate on Proverbs 3:5-7 daily: "Trust in the Lord

*with all thine heart. Lean not to thine own
understanding, but in all thy ways,
acknowledge him and he will direct thy paths."*

§

*"May the peace of God that surpasses all
understanding
guard your hearts and minds through Christ
Jesus."*

*"It is my life mission to sow the Word of God,
praying that it will land on good soil to yield,
from generation to generation, a crop of
healthy, stable and confident individuals."*
-- Elder Mae Fogle

In the Potter's hands . . .

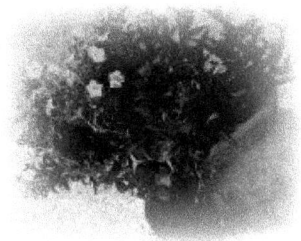

"Still, other seed fell on good soil, where it produced a crop . . ." ~ Matthew 13:8 (NIV)

www.ingramcontent.com/pod-product-compliance
Lightning Source LLC
Chambersburg PA
CBHW080404170426
43193CB00016B/2806